A TRUE BOOK™

SPACE EXPLORATION

UFOs

Jenny Mason

Children's Press®
An imprint of Scholastic Inc.

Library of Congress Cataloging-in-Publication Data
Names: Mason, Jenny (Children's author), author.
Title: UFOs/Jennifer Mason.
Other titles: True book.
Description: First edition. | New York, NY: Children's Press, an imprint of Scholastic Inc., 2022. |
  Series: A true book | Includes bibliographical references and index. | Audience: Ages 8–10. | Audience:
  Grades 4–6. | Summary: "A new set of True Books on Space Exploration"—Provided by publisher.
Identifiers: LCCN 2021041878 (print) | LCCN 2021041879 (ebook) | ISBN 9781338825947 (library binding) |
  ISBN 9781338825954 (paperback) | ISBN 9781338825961 (ebk)
Subjects: LCSH: Unidentified flying objects—Juvenile literature. | Unidentified flying objects—Sightings
  and encounters—Juvenile literature.
Classification: LCC TL789.2 .M358 2022 (print) | LCC TL789.2 (ebook) | DDC 001.942—dc23
LC record available at https://lccn.loc.gov/2021041878
LC ebook record available at https://lccn.loc.gov/2021041879

10 9 8 7 6 5 4 3 2 1   22 23 24 25 26

Printed in the U.S.A. 113
First edition, 2022

Design by Kathleen Petelinsek
Series produced by Spooky Cheetah Press

Front cover: A UFO photographed in Oregon in 1950

Back cover: A flock of starlings

Find the Truth!

Everything you are about to read is true *except* for one of the sentences on this page.

Which one is **TRUE**?

T or F Atmospheric research balloons cause the most UFO sightings during the day.

T or F Most scientists believe UFOs are spaceships piloted by aliens visiting Earth.

Find the answers in this book.

What's in This Book?

The **BIG** Truth

Looking for Extraterrestrial Life

An SR-71
Blackbird
spy plane

Is this a UFO?

3 Uncovering the Truth

4 UFO Tracking in the Future

The story of an early UFO sighting

Mysteries in the Skies

Have you ever seen a **strange object** or **weird light** in the sky? Then you have spotted a **UFO!** Any odd object or light in the sky that we cannot recognize is considered an unidentified flying object, or UFO. A UFO might also be called an **unidentified** aerial **phenomenon,** or UAP.

People have reported UFOs for **thousands of years,** though they called them by different

Auroras, which are streaks of colored light that form naturally over Earth's poles, likely caused many ancient UFO sightings.

names in the past. For instance, people from the ancient civilizations of Babylon, Assyria, China, and Mesoamerica reported **strange sightings** in texts and diaries. They described **fiery shields**, **glowing orbs**, and more. Modern science has revealed what these strange sightings really are. Though the vast majority of UFO sightings are quickly identified, a small number **remain unresolved**.

Astronomers say a supernova in 1006 CE shone about 16 times as bright as Venus.

A supernova is an extremely powerful and bright explosion of a star.

Famous Sightings

In 1006 CE, a mysterious light blazed in the night sky above Earth. It shone by day, too. People in Asia, Europe, and North America recorded the sighting. It was visible in the sky for two years before it disappeared. We now know the light came from a supernova, which is an exploding star. But early cultures did not understand outer space as we do today. To them, the light remained a wonderful mystery, or what we now call a UFO.

The Rise of Sinister UFOs

For most ancient people, strange sights in the sky were wonderful, not scary. That changed after World War II (1939–1945), which included the first use of a nuclear bomb. Many people worried about bombs falling from the sky. At the same time, stories and movies about alien invasions became popular. These circumstances led to the rise of UFO reports around the globe.

The First Flying Saucer

Does the term "UFO" cause you to imagine a flying saucer? It does for many people! This association dates back to a sighting in 1947. Kenneth Arnold often piloted his own plane when he traveled. On one trip, while flying over the Cascade Mountains in Washington State, Arnold saw nine flat curved objects zip by. News reporters called Arnold's description of the UFOs "flying saucers." No evidence of Arnold's UFOs was ever found.

A UFO sighting is sometimes called a "flap," probably because flying saucers were nicknamed "flapjacks" back in the 1950s.

FATE

SPRING 1948 25¢

VOLUME 1   NUMBER 1

THE TRUTH ABOUT THE FLYING SAUCERS
By KENNETH ARNOLD

MARK TWAIN AND HALLEY'S COMET
By HAROLD M. SHERMAN

INVISIBLE BEINGS WALK THE EARTH
By R. J. CRESCENZI

TWENTY MILLION MANIACS
By G. H. IRWIN

The FLYING DISKS

Arnold's story appeared in *Fate* magazine in 1948.

Roswell UFO Crash Site

After Arnold's sighting, a rancher near Roswell, New Mexico, told a local newspaper he had discovered a "large area of bright wreckage made up of rubber strips, tinfoil, a rather tough paper and sticks." The U.S. military claimed the debris came from a weather-tracking balloon.

Meanwhile, local rumors spread, as people claimed that the wrecked object came from outer space. And that **extraterrestrials** were on board. Although these stories were never proven to be true, Roswell became known as the UFO capital of the world.

In 1994, military documents revealed that the Roswell UFO was a secret spying balloon.

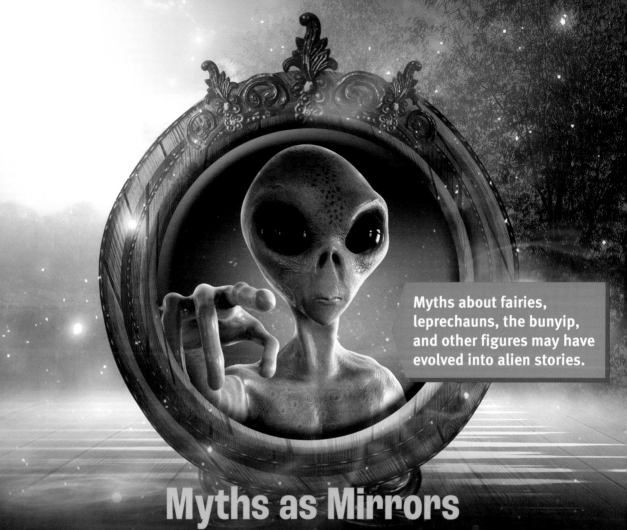

Myths about fairies, leprechauns, the bunyip, and other figures may have evolved into alien stories.

Myths as Mirrors

A common myth about UFOs is that aliens use them to come to Earth and kidnap people. Vampire, elf, and fairy stories are also common myths. Scholars refer to these shared stories as mythical patterns. Myths change as the times change. Hundreds of years ago, the stories were about elves or fairies that kidnapped people. As humankind began exploring space, people began wondering what else might be "out there." The myths shifted to alien kidnappings. Myths are like mirrors. They reflect world events.

Spy planes are basically flying cameras.

The SR-71 Blackbird's flat profile and curved surfaces hide it from radar. They also make it tough to identify as a plane!

Area 51

According to rumors, the Roswell crash debris was taken to Nevada and stashed in a secret military facility. For decades, people claimed to see more UFOs in the skies over Nevada's southern desert. Then, in 2013, the U.S. military officially admitted the existence of a top-secret base in the Nevada desert. Its code name was Area 51. Beginning in 1955, pilots there learned to fly spy planes like the U-2, the F-117 Nighthawk, and the SR-71 Blackbird. These superfast jets do look bizarre. No wonder local residents reported strange flying objects!

A Worldwide Phenomenon

UFO sightings were increasing around the world, as well. In 1980, U.S. Air Force officers chased whooshing bright lights through England's Rendlesham Forest. Investigations suggest the cause behind the UFO was a falling meteor plus an **optical illusion** created by a lighthouse.

In 1994, people across Africa reported nighttime fireballs. Astronomers later confirmed a meteor to be the cause.

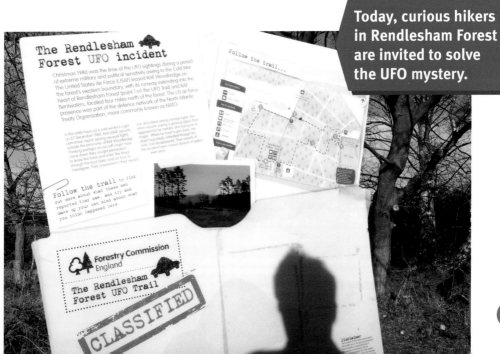

Today, curious hikers in Rendlesham Forest are invited to solve the UFO mystery.

Three Stunning UFO Videos

The most recent famous sightings were captured in three videos filmed by U.S. Navy pilots. The recorded UFOs bewildered witnesses with their speed and acrobatic motions. Investigations eventually found that the UFOs were ordinary objects. One was a weather balloon. Another was a blurry video image of a plane. The last was the heat coming off a jet engine, which can appear on video as an image or a glare. Common optical illusions made each one seem extraordinary.

Timeline of Famous UFO Sightings

1945
Sightings of foo fighters during World War II begin.

1946
Ghost rockets are seen over Sweden.

1947
Kenneth Arnold sees flying crescents in the sky, and debris from the Roswell balloon crash is found.

1954
Soccer fans see a UFO over a soccer match in Florence.

Shockwaves

The UFO videos received lots of media attention. As a result, the U.S. Congress asked the military to share all it knew about UFOs. Are they dangerous? Do they come from outer space? Do they come from enemy nations? Congress demanded a report from the Department of Defense (DOD). The DOD, also known as the Pentagon, oversees all military branches and defense intelligence agencies. In 2021, the Pentagon released its official report.

1955
The Area 51 spy plane testing facility is built, causing UFO sightings in southern Nevada to spike.

1980
Pilots chase UFOs through Rendlesham Forest, England.

1989–1990
Over the span of five months, 13,500 people in Belgium reported UFO sightings. They likely saw spy planes.

2017
The UFO videos taken by U.S. Navy pilots are leaked, leading to a DOD investigation and report.

ENTERING
AREA
51

Since 1998, NASA (the U.S. space agency) has tracked nearly 18,000 asteroids and comets known as near-Earth objects (NEOs).

Radio telescopes detect signals, weak or strong, from across the universe.

Eyes on the Skies

The Federal Aviation Administration (FAA) is the U.S. government agency that regulates air travel. The FAA and other international agencies use **satellites** to monitor almost all airspaces nearly all time. Yet, according to the 2021 Pentagon report, no single government agency is in charge of investigating UFO sightings. So what happens to all those reports from witnesses who see UFOs? And how can we ever solve UFO mysteries if no one studies the data?

Information Gaps

The 2021 report said that the DOD cannot definitively answer all of the questions about UFOs. Few of the Pentagon's military and intelligence agencies carefully analyzed or collected UFO data. And, of the ones that did, each of them used a different method for investigating UFOs. Some investigators gathered a lot of details from witnesses. Others gathered only a few facts. To make matters worse, DOD agencies rarely shared their UFO information with one another. This scattered process caused confusion and information gaps.

Inside the Report

To prepare its report to Congress, Pentagon officials reviewed 144 UFO sighting reports. The reports were made from 2004 to 2021 by military officers and staff. Some of the sightings had been recorded on video. Some had been detected on sensors such as radar and infrared cameras. Investigators were able to **debunk** only one of the UFOs. It was a deflating balloon. The other 143 cases remain unsolved.

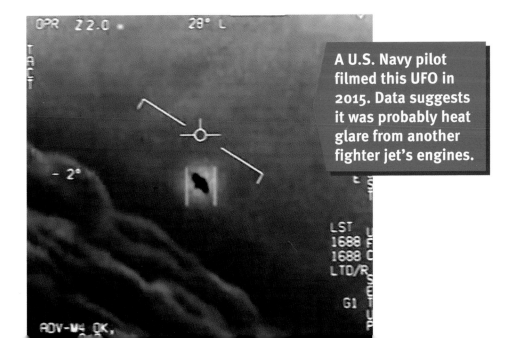

A U.S. Navy pilot filmed this UFO in 2015. Data suggests it was probably heat glare from another fighter jet's engines.

Project Blue Book

Although the Pentagon was unable to solve many UFO cases in 2021, other groups have been more successful. In 1947, the U.S. Air Force assembled the first UFO investigation team in the United States. It was eventually code-named Project Blue Book. The name came from the blue notebooks that college students used to take exams. Project Blue Book saw its UFO study as a serious exam. It investigated 12,618 sightings. Most UFOs turned out to be asteroids, airplanes, or other common objects.

FLYING SAUCERS:

AN ANALYSIS OF THE
AIR FORCE
PROJECT BLUE BOOK
SPECIAL REPORT No. 14

INCLUDING
THE C.I.A. AND THE SAUCERS
FIFTH EDITION
DECEMBER, 1976

PREPARED BY
DR. LEON DAVIDSON

Someone who studies UFOs is called a ufologist. Project Blue Book's scientists were the first ufologists.

The Right to Know

The Freedom of Information Act (FOIA) is a law that gives people the right to request information controlled by the U.S. government. Thanks to this law, we know about some of the government's secret plans to study UFOs.

The FOIA went into effect in 1967. Soon after, journalists flooded the government with requests for information about Roswell in particular and UFOs in general. Those requests revealed that the military was secretly tracking UFOs. Specifically, the North American Aerospace Defense Command (NORAD) was monitoring millions of odd objects. The agency was meant to be an alert system for enemy attacks from aircraft or outer space vehicles. If not for the FOIA—and the work of investigative journalists—the public might never have known about the 10 million UFOs NORAD tracked between the 1960s and 1980s.

NORAD is so secretive, its combat headquarters was once tucked inside a mountain.

The Secret Spies

A secret Pentagon program, called the Advanced Aerospace Threat Identification Program (AATIP), tracked UFOs from 2007 to 2012. The program's leader, Luis Elizando, resigned in 2017 and revealed the program to reporters. He said too many Pentagon officials mocked UFO sightings as silly. Rather than face ridicule, many soldiers, sailors, and military officials may have kept quiet about possible sightings.

Most of the objects that the AATIP identified were **drones** and test missiles (pictured).

France is the only European nation with a UFO investigation unit. It is called GEIPAN.

Worldwide UFO Tracking

The majority of countries do not fund UFO research or tracking. But nongovernment, or civilian, groups track UFO sightings around the world. The Mutual UFO Network (MUFON) formed in 1969. It has about 4,000 members from 43 countries. In 1974, another group, the National UFO Reporting Center (NUFORC), set up a UFO reporting hotline. Today, its website warehouses global UFO data.

Looking for Extraterrestrial Life

Many people don't believe that UFOs are caused by natural phenomena or ordinary objects. They think UFOs are actually piloted by extraterrestrials that are visiting Earth. Some people even claim to have seen aliens. If that is true, it would mean we are not alone in the universe. Most scientists do not believe these theories and stories. However, they are carrying out research to find out if there is life beyond Earth. Read on to find out about their work!

When Did the Search Start?

Life has existed on Earth for 3.5 billion years or more. By contrast, the universe is nearly 14 billion years old, yet it seems largely lifeless. In 1950, the Italian scientist Enrico Fermi challenged other scientists to solve this puzzling riddle: Does life exist anywhere in the universe besides on Earth?

Enrico Fermi

Jill Tarter

Who Is Leading the Search?

In 1984, astronomer Jill Tarter helped found the Search for Extraterrestrial Intelligence (or SETI) Institute to search for extraterrestrial life. She used radio telescopes to listen for signals and communication buzzing from faraway galaxies.

Where Is Life Likely to Be Found?

Many scientists mocked SETI until two Swiss astronomers discovered other planets besides the eight in our solar system. Known as **exoplanets**, these cosmic cousins orbit other, faraway stars. Astronomers estimate that the universe contains more planets than stars! Some exoplanets may support life, just like Earth.

Allen Telescope Array used for the SETI project

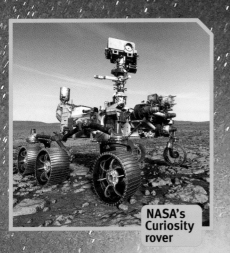
NASA's Curiosity rover

What Might Life Beyond Earth Look Like?

Scientists, including the experts at NASA, are looking for signs of life beyond Earth. In fact, that's one main goal of NASA's various Mars rover missions. In all likelihood, any life-forms found in space will not be aliens in spaceships. They will be bacteria or other tiny organisms. So while the puzzling riddle remains, we are gaining on the answer.

According to a 2017 poll, 41 million Americans have reported seeing a UFO.

The Westerbork Synthesis Radio Telescope (WSRT) searches the skies for aerial phenomena.

Uncovering the Truth

The *U* in *UFO* stands for *unidentified*. Once the object is identified, it ceases to be a UFO. Astronomers almost never report UFOs because they can identify what they see in the sky. What can we learn from the experts who study the sky? For one thing, UFOs are often found to be well-known and ordinary objects, such as clouds. To best understand the truth about UFOs, we need to look closer at the evidence.

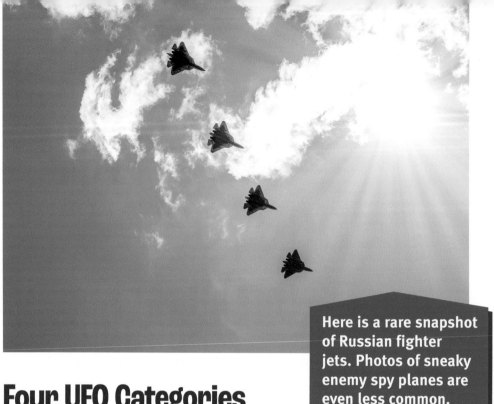

Here is a rare snapshot of Russian fighter jets. Photos of sneaky enemy spy planes are even less common.

Four UFO Categories

The 2021 Pentagon report hypothesized that all solved and unsolved UFO sightings fall into four logical categories: clutter, natural phenomena, friendly devices, and enemy technology. Tracing UFOs to enemy technologies is difficult. Military and intelligence agencies keep this information **classified**. The UFOs we know the most about are clutter, natural phenomena, and friendly devices, such as research balloons.

Clutter

From the ground, the sky may seem like a vast open space. In truth, it is rather cluttered. Trash litters the sky. Drifting plastic bags and abandoned birthday balloons have appeared as UFOs. Increasingly popular toy drones have also sparked UFO reports. And birds may outnumber all other clutter in the skies. They trigger plenty of UFO sightings.

That's no spaceship. That is a flock of birds flying in tight formation.

Every autumn, nearly nine billion birds migrate south across North America. These flocks can be mistaken for UFOs.

Natural Phenomena

Flashes and flares caused by meteors and asteroids explain many UFO sightings. These outer space rocks and boulders burn up when they enter Earth's **atmosphere**. They can look like streaking fireballs or appear as sudden bright flashes.

Sometimes sunlight reflects off the solar panels of a satellite. To people below, this reflection appears as a glowing ball that expands and shrinks. The light from a star can get distorted as it passes through hot or cold layers of air. When that happens, the starlight looks like it's jumping around.

Meteors can leave bizarre smoke trails in the sky.

Venus's bright reflection of sunlight causes the most UFO sightings at dusk.

There is a lot of junk floating in space— including tools dropped by astronauts!

Friendly Devices

Atmospheric research balloons are used to study the weather or transmit internet signals to homes. These shiny hovering objects are the most commonly reported daytime UFOs.

Old, inactive communication satellites often fall from space, sparking UFO flaps. At present, 3,000 inactive satellites orbit Earth. Some 50,000 more internet satellites will be added to Earth's orbit soon. UFO reports may spike in the future when all these machines age out of use.

A boy in India "captured" this UFO photo on his phone.

Hoaxes

Hoaxes are not included in the Pentagon's UFO report, but they fuel many UFO sightings. A hoax is a deliberate trick. Sometimes UFOs are built by people who want to fool the public. In 2009, mysterious lights over New Jersey were flashed by two teenagers. More recently, a fake photograph of a flying saucer over a city in India went viral. In 2013, a Vancouver **planetarium** disguised a drone to look like a UFO. The planetarium wanted to spark excitement for its new space exhibits.

Astronomers Stumped

In 2017, the Pan-STARRS 1 telescope in Hawaii spotted an unidentified aerial object zipping past Earth. The thin reddish slab resembled a giant hockey puck. With a diameter of 150 feet (46 meters), it was slightly larger than a blue whale. The object, which was bright and moving incredibly fast, did not look or behave like an asteroid or a comet, and it did not belong to our solar system. As a result, astronomers couldn't accurately identify it. Scientists named the object 'Oumuamua. The Hawaiian word means "scout" or "messenger." Objects from other star systems have likely visited our solar system in the past. But less advanced telescopes were not powerful enough to detect them.

Illustration of 'Oumuamua

'Oumuamua may have traveled to our solar system from the Vega star system. That's a distance of about 25 light-years, or 146 trillion miles (236 trillion kilometers).

Like UFOs, no two stars are alike. They all differ in size, temperature, composition, and brightness.

Trillions of stars flood the universe. New stars are born in murky gas and dust clouds like the Carina Nebula (pictured).

UFO Tracking in the Future

Tracking UFO data is very difficult. Descriptions of sightings vary greatly. And the information is disorganized. Scientists faced a similar problem in the 1880s when they were trying to sort all the stars in the universe. Astronomer Annie Jump Cannon came up with a simplified system. She classified stars by their color and their temperature. Similarly, scientists today can use computers to categorize UFOs.

AI to the Rescue

UFO investigators are hopeful that artificial intelligence (AI) software can help them solve all UFO mysteries. AI has the power to quickly find patterns in a heap of information. In some instances, AI could sift through decades of UFO data caught on radar. Whenever new UFOs appear on radar systems, the software could compare the new mystery to previously debunked cases.

AI's sorting process is similar to the method detectives use to match crime-scene fingerprints to prints stored in a database.

A World Without UFOs

Improved UFO tracking is a safety issue. Some UFOs pose risks to pilots and air passengers. That danger spreads to the wider public if UFOs can be traced back to enemy nations or terrorists. Advances in technology make it easy to imagine a future where UFO reports cease altogether. Imagine a smartphone app that can instantly debunk any hovering object or bizarre light in the sky! But will such a world be less wondrous with every UFO mystery solved? Probably not. Even with every star categorized, the universe inspires awe and wonder.

Debunk UFO Mysteries

Scientists conduct experiments and study data to find answers. See if you can you debunk these UFO mysteries like a scientist would. Study each picture and consider the clues carefully. Use background knowledge you've gained from this book.

1 Clue: A string of glowing balls that got bigger and smaller was seen rising up from the horizon.

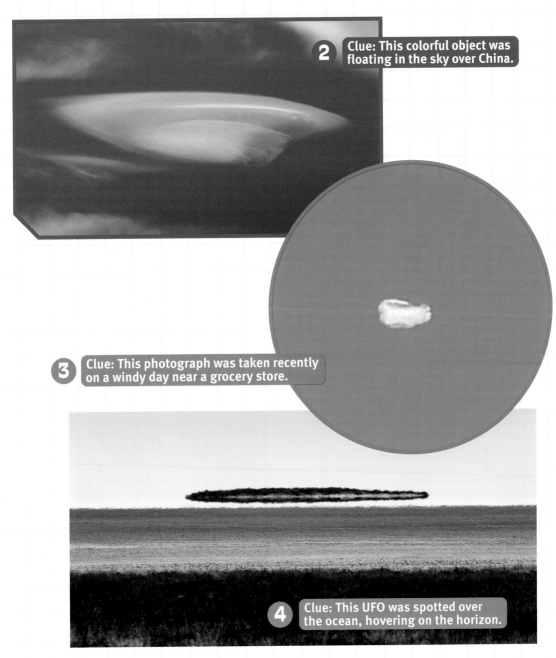

2 Clue: This colorful object was floating in the sky over China.

3 Clue: This photograph was taken recently on a windy day near a grocery store.

4 Clue: This UFO was spotted over the ocean, hovering on the horizon.

ANSWERS: 1. Sunlight reflecting off an array of satellites. 2. A cloud. 3. A shopping bag. 4. A rare optical illusion that can be caused by the way light is bent by the atmosphere.

Create an Optical Illusion

Many UFO sightings result from optical illusions—when our brains misinterpret what we see. Is seeing believing? You can find out by making some optical illusions!

Materials

Paper

Markers

An empty recycled cereal or cracker box

Tape

A clear glass container

Water

Directions

1 On one sheet of paper, use a marker to draw two big arrows. Make sure they are pointing in the same direction.

4 Experiment with more optical illusions on separate pieces of paper. Draw two arrows pointing in opposite directions. What happens when you view the arrows through the water?

2 Tape the sheet of paper to the empty box and set it upright on a table.

3 Place the empty glass container about 9 inches (23 centimeters) in front of the arrows. Gradually fill the container with water. Observe what happens to the arrows when you view them through the water.

5 You can also experiment with patterns. Fill one sheet of paper with different-colored stripes or a multicolored grid. What happens when you slide the glass container full of water across your view of the stripes or patterns?

What Happened?

Our eyes require light to perceive the world. Light bends, or refracts, when it passes through water. Refraction changes what we see. It makes the arrows and patterns you drew look different when they are seen through the water.

43

True Statistics

U.S. state with the most UFO sightings per person: Idaho

Total spent by AATIP over 5 years investigating UFOs: $22,000,000

The percentage of Americans who had heard of flying saucers by 1966: 96%

The average number of new asteroids and comets NASA discovers weekly: 40

European country with the most UFO sightings in 2020: Ireland

The trend in UFO sightings from 2014 to 2018: 59% decrease

The average number of satellites crashing to Earth each week: 1

The estimated number of members in Australia's many UFO fan clubs: 1,000

Did you find the truth?

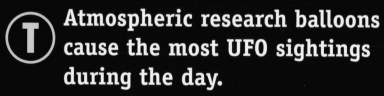

T Atmospheric research balloons cause the most UFO sightings during the day.

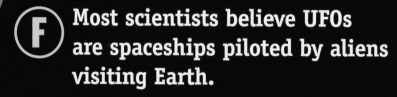

F Most scientists believe UFOs are spaceships piloted by aliens visiting Earth.

Resources

Other books in this series:

 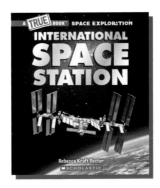 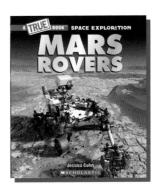

You can also look at:

Hile, Lori. *Aliens and UFOs: Myth or Reality?* North Mankato, MN: Capstone Press, 2018.

Hulick, Kathryn. *Strange but True: 10 of the World's Greatest Unexplained Mysteries Explained*. London: Frances Lincoln Children's Books, 2019.

Manzanero, Paula. *Where Is Area 51?* New York: Penguin Workshop, 2018.

Glossary

atmosphere (AT-muhs-feer) the mixture of gases that surrounds a planet

classified (KLAS-uh-fide) declared secret by the government

debunk (dee-BUNK) expose what is false

drones (drohnz) aircraft without pilots that are controlled remotely

exoplanets (EK-soh-plan-its) planets that orbit a star outside our solar system

extraterrestrial (ek-struh-tuh-RES-tree-uhl) coming from a place beyond Earth or beyond our solar system

optical illusion (AHP-ti-kuhl i-LOO-zhuhn) something that tricks the eye by seeming to be what it is not

phenomenon (fuh-NAH-muh-nahn) an event or a fact that can be seen or felt, sometimes something very unusual and remarkable

planetarium (plan-i-TAIR-ee-uhm) a building with equipment for reproducing the position and movements of the sun, moon, planets, and stars by projecting their images onto a curved ceiling

satellite (SAT-uh-lite) a spacecraft, a moon, or another heavenly body that travels in an orbit around a larger heavenly body

Index

Page numbers in **bold** indicate illustrations.

About the Author

Jenny Mason is a story-hunter. She explores foreign countries, canyon mazes, and burial crypts to gather the facts that make the best true tales. She interviews everyone from roboticists to NASA engineers. Her research knows no bounds. She once tracked sand-burrowing worms on a stormy beach and sniffed a 200-year-old rotten skull. Jenny received an MFA in Writing for Children and Young Adults from the Vermont College of Fine Arts. She also holds an MPhil from Trinity College Dublin. When not researching or writing, she performs and produces Blister & Muck, The Unsolvable Mystery Podcast, at blisterandmuck.com.